MW01156082

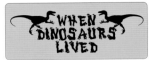

GIANTS OF THE SKY

BY "DINO" DON LESSEM

ILLUSTRATED BY
JOHN BINDON

For Spencer—D.L.

For Hall. Thanks for your neverending dinosaur factoids
and insights.—J.B.

Copyright © 2002 by Don Lessem. Illustrations copyright © 2002 by John Bindon. All rights
reserved. Published by Grosset & Dunlap, a division of Penguin Putnam Books for Young
Readers, New York. GROSSET & DUNLAP is a trademark of Penguin Putnam Inc.
Published simultaneously in Canada. Printed in China.

Library of Congress Cataloging-in-Publication Data is available.

ISBN 0-448-42647-1   A B C D E F G H I J

A WORD FROM DINO DON

Even before dinosaurs walked the earth, the first flying reptiles appeared in the sky. We call them pterosaurs (TERR-oh-sores), which means "winged reptiles." The first pterosaurs were the size of crows, and they lived more than 230 million years ago. During the 170 million years before they disappeared, there were hundreds of different pterosaurs. Some were very strange, with oddly shaped tails, skulls, and teeth.

No animal that has flown before or since grew as big as the largest pterosaurs. By the end of dinosaur time, some had grown as wide as fighter planes. And then, 65 million years ago, the pterosaurs were gone. They disappeared at the same time, and just as mysteriously, as the dinosaurs. But from fossil discoveries, we are still learning about the many strange giants who once ruled the skies. I think you'll love the animals you'll meet here—I do!

'Dino' Don
Lessem

DINO DON SAYS: Pterosaurs were NOT dinosaurs, although they lived together. Saying a pterosaur is a kind of dinosaur is like calling a bat a kind of elephant. Sure, they are both mammals, but there isn't much else they have in common.

TINY FLIERS

Swooping low over an ancient landscape, a hungry flier searches for an insect meal. Meet *Peteinosaurus* (PEH-teen-OH-sore-us), one of the first flying reptiles. It probably developed from reptiles that climbed trees! Even *Peteinosaurus* may have clung to branches with its long fingers.

DINO DON SAYS: How do we know Peteinosaurus *ate insects? We don't! But it only had a few simple cone-shaped teeth in its jaws, so it may have lived on insects, which it could swallow whole. Its teeth just weren't built for catching or biting anything large.*

PTEROFACTS

Peteinosaurus

MEANING OF NAME: "winged lizard"

PLACE: Northern Italy

TIME: 225 million years ago, Triassic

SIZE: up to 2 feet wide

DIET: insects

YEAR NAMED: 1978

PTEROFACTS

Dimorphodon

MEANING OF NAME: "two-toothed form"
PLACE: England, Mexico
TIME: 200 million years ago, Early Jurassic
SIZE: up to 5 feet wide
DIET: insects
YEAR NAMED: 1859

LEARNING TO EAT

Long-tailed pterosaurs cling to a cliff's edge, watching the sea. They are looking out for fish to eat—and for giant sea reptiles that might eat them!

These are *Dimorphodon* (DI-mor-fo-DON), big-headed pterosaurs first found in England. They were small compared to later pterosaurs, but they were still strong fliers. They would glide powerfully just above the surface of the water, dipping their heads down to snag fish.

DINO DON SAYS: "She sold sea shells by the seashore." Do you know that tongue twister? It may be about an actual young lady. Mary Anning found many fossils as well as shells on the British sea coast nearly 200 years ago. From the age of twelve, she supported her family and became famous for her finds, including the first skeleton of a Dimorphodon, which she found in the 1820s.

BATTLE FOR BREAKFAST

Grabbing lunch is a battle in the sky over Europe, 160 million years ago! *Angustinaripterus* (AN-gus-teen-ah-RIP-terr-us) snatches a fish from the smaller *Rhamphorhynchus* (RAM-for-ink-US).

Though it was just a foot wide across its wings, *Rhamphorhynchus* was one of the most common and long-lasting of all the early pterosaurs. It fed on small fish that it snatched up in its pointy beak.

But it's no match for *Angustinaripterus*, a long-headed animal three times its width. *Angustinaripterus* was a powerful flier, even though it had only a stumpy tail. Its top and bottom teeth alternated spaces, creating a powerful gripping bite.

DINO DON SAYS: Rhamphorhynchus *had 20 top teeth and 14 lower teeth.* Angustinaripterus *had more teeth on the bottom—up to 20 teeth. On its top jaws, it had just 18 teeth. And its nose was unusually narrow, too.*

PTEROFACTS

Angustinaripterus
MEANING OF NAME: "narrow-nostriled wing" (the nostrils are not on the wing!)
PLACE: China
TIME: 160 million years ago, Late Jurassic
SIZE: up to 3 feet wide
DIET: fish
YEAR NAMED: 1983

PTEROFACTS

Rhamphorhynchus
MEANING OF NAME: "beaked snout"
PLACE: Germany
TIME: 145 million years ago, Late Jurassic Period
SIZE: up to 5.5 feet wide
DIET: fish
YEAR NAMED: 1847

DINO DON SAYS: *Nearly 300 skeletons of* Pterodactylus *have been found beautifully preserved in the limestone of Eichstatt, Germany. They were buried in the soft dust at the bottom of ancient poisonous lagoons. The smallest is a baby just 7 inches long and perhaps only five weeks old.*

PTEROFACTS

Pterodactylus
MEANING OF NAME: "wing finger"
PLACE: Germany
TIME: 145 million years ago, Late Jurassic
SIZE: up to 8 feet wide
DIET: fish
YEAR NAMED: 1815

NEW RULERS OF THE SKY

Waves crash as a giant sea reptile leaps from the water, frightening a colony of pelican-sized pterodactyls high in the nearby trees.

Pterodactylus (TERR-oh-DAK-till-US) was the first of the short-tailed fliers discovered in modern times. This kind of wide-bodied pterosaur appeared late in the Jurassic Period, at nearly the same time as the first birds. But pterodactyls, not birds, ruled the skies until the end of dinosaur time.

STRANGE TEETH

These pterosaurs are standing, shaking their heads and comb-like teeth in the water. What are they doing?

Most pterosaurs snagged fish in their sharp teeth while flying along the surface of the water. But some pterosaurs had teeth more like combs, like these *Pterodaustro* (TERR-oh-DOW-stroh).

Inside their mouths were nearly 1,000 teeth arranged like delicate combs. They used them to sift tiny animals out of the water and into their mouths. Through these combs, the pterosaurs then spat out the water, trapping and swallowing the bugs.

Gnathosaurus (NAY-tho-SORE-us) from Europe ate the same way, although it had many less teeth. And so did *Ctenochasma* (KUH-ten-oh-CAZ-ma), who looked like *Gnathosaurus* but with fewer teeth in its mouth—"only" 150!

PTEROFACTS

Pterodaustro
MEANING OF NAME: "south wing"
PLACE: Argentina
TIME: 110 million years ago, Early Cretaceous
SIZE: up to 4.5 feet wide
DIET: insects, small water animals
YEAR NAMED: 1969

DINO DON SAYS: Gnathosaurus *means "awl-teeth." It is named this because its pointy teeth are shaped like the screwdriver-like tool called an awl. The scientific names of pterosaurs, like those of most animals, come from Greek and Latin. That's why some of them can be so hard for us to pronounce!*

FLIERS ON LAND

We're on a beach in China, 140 million years ago. Coming toward us is a huge strange-headed flier. It swoops down to waddle after a large crab and crushes it on the bony knobs in the back of its jaws. This is *Dsungaripterus* (ZUNG-a-RIP-terr-us).

It may also have used its oddly pointed and curved jaws to dig for small water animals. For many pterosaurs, fish were not the only source of food, and water was not the only place to feed.

DINO DON SAYS: Many pterosaurs had head crests as weird as Dsungaripterus's. *We don't know the purpose of these bony growths. Maybe they served as rudders, like those on the tails of the more primitive pterosaurs. Or perhaps they were just for display to attract mates, or even to help make sounds.*

PTEROFACTS

Dsungaripterus

MEANING OF NAME: "Junggar Basin wing"

PLACE: Africa and Xinjiang, China

TIME: 140 million years ago, Early Cretaceous

SIZE: up to 10 feet wide

DIET: small water animals, fish, shellfish

YEAR NAMED: 1964

BRINGING UP BABY

Ornithocheirus (OR-nith-oh-KY-russ) is bringing live squid to its young for a tasty breakfast! This long-jawed pterosaur was probably a fish-eater. Perhaps it stored fish for itself and its young in a throat pouch like that of pelicans today. This adult is 8 feet long, but new finds suggest *Ornithocheirus* may have grown to more than 40 feet wide—larger than any other flying animal!

How did most pterosaurs care for their babies? They probably laid small eggs in nests, whether in trees, on sheltered spots along the shore, or on the edge of cliffs. The newly hatched young would have been small and probably unable to fly at first. They had little teeth and big eyes. As warm-blooded animals, they must have needed a lot of food to grow quickly and stay warm.

DINO DON SAYS:
Ornithocheirus *means "bird hand." A nice name, but its hand wasn't bird-like at all! Like other pterosaurs, it had four fingers on each hand. The fourth finger helped form the long frame for its wing.*

PTEROFACTS

Ornithocheirus
MEANING OF NAME:
"bird hand"
PLACE: England, Australia
TIME: 100 million years ago, Early Cretaceous
SIZE: up to 43 feet wide
DIET: fish
YEAR NAMED: 1869

FANCY HEADS

Some pterosaurs had huge crests on the front of their snouts. *Anhanguera* (AN-han-GERR-a) was one of the largest of these—about as wide as a city street! Not quite as large, and without the crest, is its opponent in this fish-fight: *Caeradactylus* (SERR-a-DACK-till-us).

        Caeradactylus may have been smaller, but it had unusually strong teeth that were spoon-shaped in front to help grip fish. So this time, the smaller pterosaur may actually have won the battle for food.

PTEROFACTS

Anhanguera
MEANING OF NAME: "old devil"
PLACE: Brazil
TIME: 100 million years ago, EarlyCretaceous
SIZE: up to 19 feet wide
DIET: fish
YEAR NAMED: 1985

DINO DON SAYS: *The fancy crest on the head of* Anhanguera *might have helped to keep its head still while it flew. Another theory is that the hollow crests might also have been used to make sounds. We don't know if that's true about pterosaurs. Duck-billed dinosaurs probably did use their crests to honk!*

PTEROFACTS

Caeradactylus
MEANING OF NAME: "Caera-finger"
PLACE: Brazil
TIME: 100 million years ago, Early Cretaceous
SIZE: up to 18 feet wide
DIET: fish
YEAR NAMED: 1985

SHARING THE SKY

Look up! There are many different pterosaurs in the skies. Like birds today, several kinds of pterosaurs could live in the same time and place. With their different sizes, shapes, and strategies for feeding, they were able to share a home.

Tropeognathus (TROH-pee-oh-guh-NAY-thus) was a huge fish-eater. It is easily recognized by its bizarre head, with weird bony crests on both its top and bottom jaws.

Tupuxuara (TOO-puh-SHU-wear-uh) had no teeth at all. It is not as well known as its cousin, *Tapajara* (TAP-a-JAIR-uh), which was also toothless with a strangely bird-like beak. We don't know what these toothless pterosaurs ate—maybe insects, eggs, or soft-shelled sea creatures.

PTEROFACTS

Tupuxuara
MEANING OF NAME: "familiar spirit"
PLACE: Brazil
TIME: 100 million years ago, Early Cretaceous
SIZE: up to 20 feet wide
DIET: fish
YEAR NAMED: 1988

DINO DON SAYS: Tupuxuara *and* Tapajara *are both named for mytho-logical creatures in the language of the Tupi tribe of Brazil.*

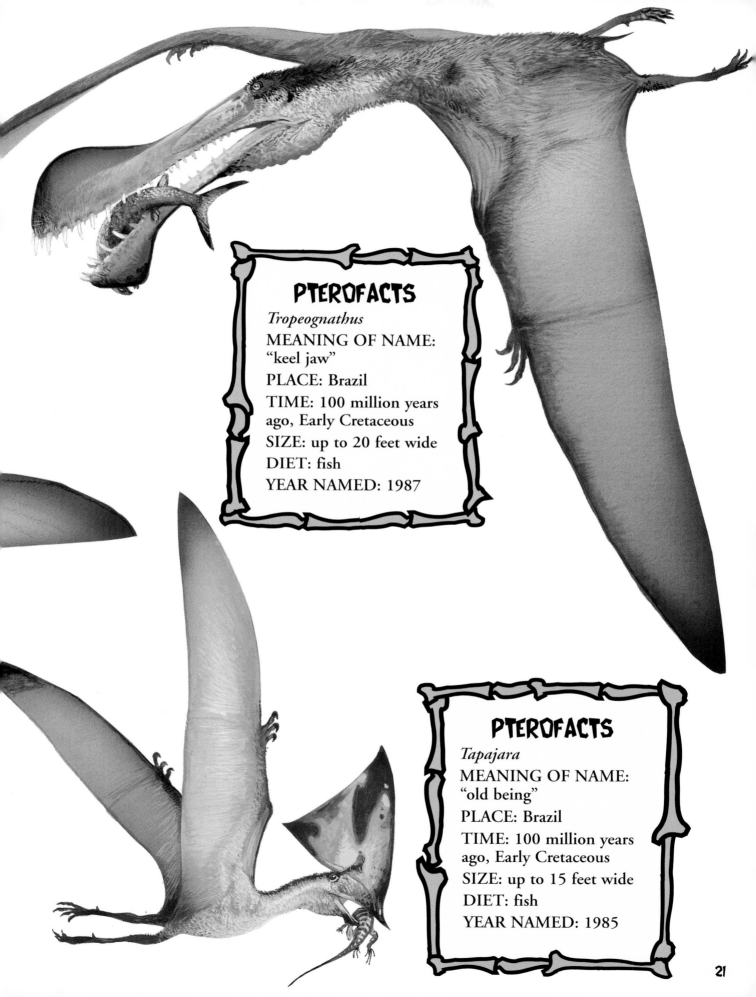

PTEROFACTS

Tropeognathus

MEANING OF NAME: "keel jaw"

PLACE: Brazil

TIME: 100 million years ago, Early Cretaceous

SIZE: up to 20 feet wide

DIET: fish

YEAR NAMED: 1987

PTEROFACTS

Tapajara

MEANING OF NAME: "old being"

PLACE: Brazil

TIME: 100 million years ago, Early Cretaceous

SIZE: up to 15 feet wide

DIET: fish

YEAR NAMED: 1985

DANGER IN THE SEA

Look out below! *Liopleurodon* (LIE-oh-PLOOR-oh-don), a sea reptile even bigger than the fighter-plane sized *Pteranodon* (TERR-an-oh-DON), is ready to attack the pterosaur if it dives for a fish. Even for a huge pterosaur like *Pteranodon*, the sea is not a safe place to feed. Without teeth, it has few defenses other than its sharp beak.

Pteranodon was one of the last of the pterosaurs. It lived in the American Midwest—but on the ocean! Eighty million years ago, Kansas was under a large sea that stretched north to south through the middle of North America. A powerful flier, *Pteranodon* may have roamed widely across the sea to find safe places to feed.

DINO DON SAYS: How do you tell a boy pterosaur from a girl? We're not sure from the fossils we have. But it seems that some pterosaurs (including many Pteranodons) differed from each other mainly in their crests. So maybe you could tell males and females apart by the size of their bony "hats."

22

THE BIGGEST FLIERS

One of the biggest animals ever to fly—*Quetzalcoatlus* (KETT-sall-koh-AT-luss)—is on the hunt! The giant grabs a fish . . . and the wading bird, *Hesperornis* (HESS-pur-OR-niss), that was eating it! Its wings cast a shadow four times wider than condors, the largest birds alive today.

Could a flier so enormous really snag fish like this? We don't know. How and what *Quetzalcoatlus* ate is a mystery. It lived in the American West after the sea in that region had dried up. So how did *Quetzalcoatlus* find food so far from an ocean?

Perhaps with its great wings it could fly very far to find water and fish. Or maybe it was a scavenger who ate animals that died on land. But *Quetzalcoatlus* had no teeth and a narrow beak—so it would not have had much strength for tearing food. Maybe floods sweeping across its land made pools of water that attracted crabs and other shellfish that *Quetzalcoatlus* could have eaten.

DINO DON SAYS: Quetzalcoatlus was one of the last of all the pterosaurs, living very near the end of dinosaur time.

PTEROFACTS

Quetzalcoatlus
MEANING OF NAME: "feathered serpent"
PLACE: American West
TIME: 65 million years ago, Late Cretaceous
SIZE: up to 45 feet wide
DIET: fish, small animals
YEAR NAMED: 1975

FINDING FOSSIL TREASURE

How are pterosaurs found? Often fossils are discovered by accident! In the early 1970s, a college student was out walking in the badlands of western Texas. In the bottom of a dried-out valley, the student saw some bone fragments. He looked up higher and found a mysterious three-feet-long bone sticking out of the rock. He dug it out and took it to his professor, Dr. Wann Langston, Jr.

Dr. Langston recognized the bone as a pterosaur wing. After months of patient searching and digging, Dr. Langston and his assistants found hundreds of bones. Almost all of them belonged to one wing of a huge pterosaur—an animal up to 50 feet wide. That is as wide as a fighter plane! The bones belonged to *Quetzalcoatlus*. Dr. Langston named it after a god in ancient Aztec Indian mythology.

DINO DON SAYS: *Pterosaurs are very light.* *Engineers have estimated that* Quetzalcoatlus *weighed just 220 pounds—no more than a couch, though it was as wide as a basketball court!*

HOW DID THEY FLY?

A *Pteranodon* pushes off from a cliff. It flaps its huge wings and glides out over the water. Sounds easy, right?

Actually, it requires a complicated arrangement of bones and muscles. All pterosaurs had short upper arms attached to a hook-shaped shoulder bone. In *Pteranodon* and other large pterosaurs, the shoulder is linked to the chest and its powerful muscles in much the same way as in modern birds. As the wings flapped, the shoulder turned to change the wing position.

But what is unusual about a pterosaur is that its wing skeleton is made of a single long, thin bone, and not a network of several bones like those of birds today. This bone stretches the wing membrane from the animal's wrist, through its fourth finger, and into the shoulder.

DINO DON SAYS: *Some pterosaurs had hair! They were warm-blooded animals that used a lot of energy to fly, so hair might have helped to keep them warm.*

PTEROFACTS

Scientists don't know whether pterosaurs could run, or just waddle, on land. A lot depends on where their wings attached—to their ankles or higher on their legs. New fossil finds from Germany suggest that at least some pterosaurs waddled on all fours with webbed toes!

OTHER FLIERS

Long before and after pterosaurs, there were other strange, amazing, and sometimes huge creatures in the air. *Meganeura* (MEG-ah-NURE-ah) was a dragonfly-like insect from the Carboniferous swamp forests of 325 million years ago. Among the largest of all flying insects, it grew to 2 feet in width, as wide as a refrigerator!

Only one mammal has learned to fly: the bat. *Icaronycteris* (ICK-care-oon-ICK-terr-iss) is the earliest known bat from North America. It flew in search of insects perhaps 35 million years ago.

And, of course, birds are today's living relatives of the dinosaurs. But the largest of all flying birds, *Argentinavis* (AR-gen-TEEN-ave-is), lived three million years ago and had a wingspan of more than 20 feet. Huge as it was, some pterosaurs grew twice as large!

DINO DON SAYS: Why did the pterosaurs disappear? Pterosaurs, dinosaurs, giant marine reptiles, and many other animals died out 65 million years ago. Maybe an asteroid crash changed the weather so they couldn't survive. But it appears many of these animals were already on their way out, perhaps because of slower climate changes.

Meganeura

Icaronycteris

Argentinavis

MESOZOIC ERA millions of years ago

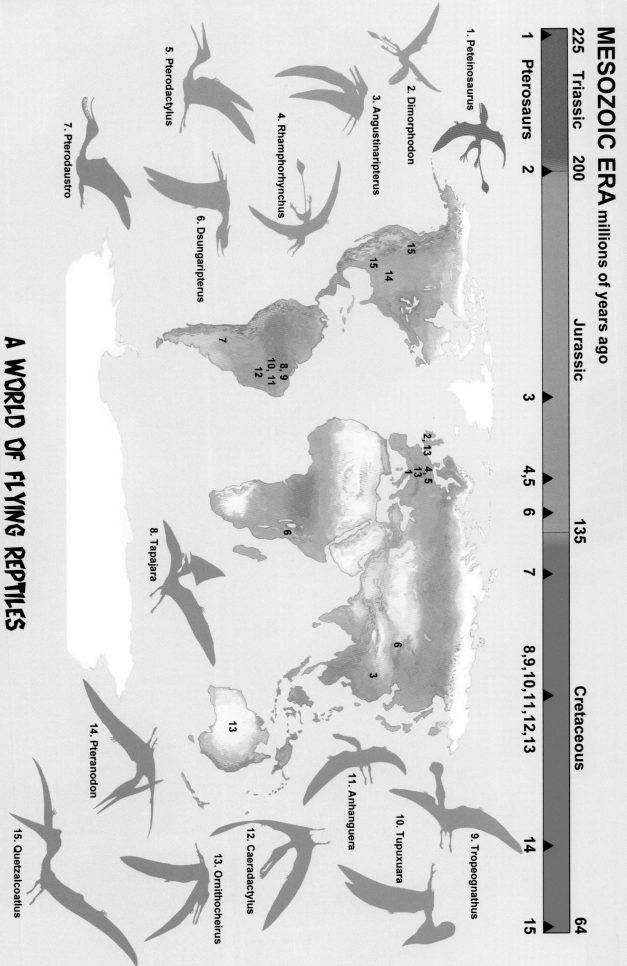

225	200		135		64
Triassic		Jurassic		Cretaceous	

Pterosaurs
1   2   3   4,5   6   7   8,9,10,11,12,13   14   15

1. Peteinosaurus
2. Dimorphodon
3. Angustinaripterus
4. Rhamphorhynchus
5. Pterodactylus
6. Dsungaripterus
7. Pterodaustro
8. Tapajara
9. Tropeognathus
10. Tupuxuara
11. Anhanguera
12. Caeradactylus
13. Ornithocheirus
14. Pteranodon
15. Quetzalcoatlus

A WORLD OF FLYING REPTILES

Pterosaurs lived everywhere there was water, from before there were dinosaurs to very near their end. We know of more than 100 kinds of pterosaurs so far, but hundreds more probably flew. This map shows you where we've found fossils so far of the flying reptiles featured in this book.